DATE		
FEB 7 1984	FEB 23 '95	
	FEB 27 '96	
FEB 16 1985		
FEB 21 1985	FEB 06 '97	
FE 17 '86	FEB 26 '97	
FE 12 '87	FEB 08 '99	
DE 3 '87	AG 11 '99	
JY 28 '88	FE 15 '03	
FE 2 '89	FE 22 '05	
FE 24 '90		
FE 25 '93		

VALENTINE'S DAY

♥

FERN G. BROWN

VALENTINE'S DAY

FRANKLIN WATTS
New York / London / Toronto / Sydney / 1983
A FIRST BOOK

Acknowledgments

A special thank you to Hallmark Cards, Incorporated,
for their splendid cooperation.
For manuscript assistance, thank you to:
Betsy Barnett, Cristi Barnett, Blaine Barnett,
Allison Brown, Marni Brown, Stacey Brown,
Marsha Brown, and Minna Goldberg.

Illustrations by Anne Canevari Green

Photographs courtesy of:
Monkmeyer Photo Service: opp. p. 1;
New York Public Library Picture Collection:
pp. 12, 20, 24, 29, 36;
Hallmark Cards, Inc.: pp. 15, 30, 33, 34.

Library of Congress Cataloging in Publication Data

Brown, Fern.
Valentine's Day.

(A First book)
Includes index.
Bibliography: p.
Summary: Traces the legendary origins of the holiday
celebrated in modern times as the special day of lovers,
as well as the history since 1800 of the valentine card.
Includes recipes and games for a valentine party.
1. Saint Valentine's Day—Juvenile literature.
[1. Valentine's Day. 2. Valentines] I. Green, Anne
Canevari, ill. II. Title.
GT4925.B76 1983   394.2'683   82-16090
ISBN 0-531-04533-1

CONTENTS

To My Valentine
L.J.B.
Forever 'n' Ever
F.

1

VALENTINE'S DAY BEGINNINGS

Pink and red hearts, chubby cupids, and lace-trimmed valentine boxes filled to overflowing tell us it's Valentine's Day. Each year on February 14 people celebrate this light-hearted holiday by exchanging tokens of love and friendship called valentines.

The valentine may be a greeting card, a box of candy, a bouquet of flowers, or something to wear. It might be funny or romantic. But for thousands of years the message has been the same. "I'm thinking of you." "I'm your friend." "I love you."

Why is February 14 called St. Valentine's Day, and how did the holiday begin? No one is absolutely sure. Valentine's Day seems to be a mixture of customs, legends, beliefs, and superstitions that have been handed down from one generation to the next.

Valentine's Day was named after St. Valentine, a Christian priest. There were several priests with that name, but the Valentine we know best, lived in Rome in the third century after Christ. At that time, most Romans worshipped many different gods and did not accept the relatively new Christian religion. Christians were persecuted and forbidden to worship as they pleased. Valentine was executed on February 14 for preaching Christianity. He was later proclaimed a saint.

Why is St. Valentine thought of as the patron saint, or special guardian of lovers? According to one legend, Emperor Claudius II of ancient Rome was badly in need of an army. He thought that married men wouldn't make good soldiers, because they wouldn't want to leave their wives and children to fight wars. So he issued an unheard-of order forbidding young men to marry. It said that any priest who performed a marriage ceremony would be put to death!

According to the legend, a priest named Valentine disobeyed the Emperor and performed secret marriages for young couples. He was thrown into prison and beheaded for his crime on February 14. Some people believe that Valentine's Day is celebrated because Valentine, a priest, believed in love.

Others say, that in the language of the Norman French in the Middle Ages, the word *galantin*, which means lover of women, sounded like "Valentin." These similar sounding words may have made people think St. Valentine was the patron saint of lovers.

Another story tells of a priest named Valentine who loved children and gave them flowers from his garden. He was put in prison by the emperor because he refused to pray to Roman gods.

The children missed their friend and threw him bouquets of flowers with love notes attached, through the prison bars. Valentine spent a year in prison with only the bare necessities. He became fond of the jailer's blind daughter, who brought him messages and food and tried to make life a little easier for him.

When Valentine was commanded to appear before Claudius II, the Emperor was impressed with the priest's gentleness and dignity. Claudius offered to set Valentine free if he would give up his religion and worship the Roman gods.

Valentine refused. Then he did a daring thing. He tried to convert the Emperor to Christianity! Claudius went into a rage and ordered Valentine put to death.

During his last days, the brave priest prayed for a miracle for the jailer's daughter, and she regained her sight. Before Valentine died, he wrote her a farewell message and signed it, "From your Valentine."

Valentine was beheaded. Some people say that on February 14, the anniversary of his death, we send valentines, flowers, or love notes in his memory.

Still another legend traces Valentine's Day to an ancient Roman festival, the Lupercalia. February 14, the day Valentine died, happened to be the eve of this important holiday. At that time, the Roman calendar was different from the one we use today. The month of February came later in the year, and Lupercalia was a spring holiday.

Long before Valentine lived, when Rome was only a shepherd's village, people celebrated Lupercalia on February 15. They honored Lupercus, the god of herds and crops, with games, songs, and dancing. They believed that Lupercus protected their flocks from wolves and kept them and their animals fertile and healthy.

Name-drawing was a favorite custom in Rome during Lupercalia. Young women wrote their names on pieces of paper and put them into an urn or bowl. On Lupercalia eve each young man drew a name. The girl whose name he drew became his partner at the dances and parties for the coming year. Sometimes they became sweethearts and were married before the next name-drawing. We don't know when or how the custom started.

Through the years, more Romans became Christians. Priests were no longer put to death for teaching the religion. The church tried to abolish pagan holidays like Lupercalia. But the people enjoyed the old festivals and their traditions. Lupercalia went on until late in the fifth century.

The priests then changed the festival's name to St. Valentine's Day and moved the date to February 14, the day Valentine died. This happy spring celebration no longer honored the Roman god Lupercus. It now was more of a Christian holiday. But people wouldn't give up the ancient traditions of Lupercalia. St. Valentine's Day was still thought of as a celebration of fertility and love.

Sorting out St. Valentine's Day fact from legend isn't easy. The stories about the brave Christian priests are inspiring examples of friendship and love. Perhaps they are the reasons we send affectionate messages to our friends and loved ones each February 14.

2

VALENTINE CUSTOMS OF LONG AGO

Rome grew from a small village to a great walled city. The mighty Roman army conquered most of Europe, and the soldiers who occupied Britain brought the Roman holidays and customs with them.

After a time, the English began celebrating the Roman holidays. They even had name-drawings on St. Valentine's Day. The holiday itself may have come from the Romans, but the celebrations were filled with English customs and traditions.

In England, birds returned from the south in February. Partridges and blackbirds built nests around the time of Valentine's Day, in preparation for having a family and raising their young. Many women thought about love and marriage when the birds nested. So, on Valentine's Day they used magic spells and charms to predict who their husbands would be.

If a young girl in Derbyshire county in England wanted a husband, she'd practice this bit of magic. On St. Valentine's eve at midnight, she'd circle the church, scatter a handful of hemp-seed and chant:

I sow a hempseed,
Hempseed I sow.
He that loves me best,
Come after and mow.

Then, she'd run toward home, peeking over her shoulder. If a young man was following her, she believed they'd be married before the end of the year.

On the night before Valentine's Day, one English girl pinned four bay leaves to the corners of her pillow, and a fifth to the center. She thought that green leaves stood for hope for lovers, and that if she dreamed of her sweetheart, she'd be married that year. To make certain that she would dream of him, she hard-boiled an egg, peeled it, and saved the shell. Then she took out the yolk and filled it with salt. Before she went to bed, she ate the egg, shell and all. She didn't speak or drink all night.

Another girl had the idea that the first boy she saw on Valentine's Day would become her husband. She kept her eyes closed all morning until her sweetheart came to visit.

Other English girls wrote boys' names on scraps of paper. They rolled each paper in a small piece of clay and dropped the clay into the water. The clay fell away, and the girls believed that the first paper to surface held the name of their future husband.

English children, too, celebrated Valentine's Day. They

went from house to house in groups singing songs and chanting verses like this one:

Good morning, Valentine;
Curl your locks as I do mine
Two before and three behind
Good morning, Valentine
Hurrah! Hurrah! Hurrah!

Many times, people threw flower wreaths or pennies to them.

The celebration of Valentine's Day spread to other countries. In time, most of Europe had special rites and ceremonies to honor St. Valentine.

In Italy, during the Middle Ages, men and women gathered in flower gardens and listened to romantic music and poetry on St. Valentine's Day. Then they found partners and walked through the gardens. But eventually this pleasant custom died out and traditional St. Valentine's Day celebrations disappeared in Italy.

If a German girl wanted to know who her husband would be she would plant onions in pots on St. Valentine's Day. Each onion was tagged with the name of a boy and the pot was placed near the fireplace. The girl believed that she would marry the boy whose name was attached to the first onion to sprout.

Later, in Germany, Austria, and Hungary, the church frowned on such St. Valentine's Day customs and tried to change them. At the name-drawings, names of saints were substituted for girls' names. Boys were supposed to live the life of the saint whose name they'd drawn for a year. Name-drawing lost its popularity, probably because of this change. Valentine's Day celebrations in these countries died out.

In the early 1600s wealthy people in France often gave valentine parties. Madame Royale, a French princess, named her palace, "The Valentine," and gave lavish parties. There were name-drawings, and each gentleman gave his lady flowers. He was supposed to give her flowers at every dance that year.

Valentine parties and fancy-dress balls became more frequent in England and France. On these festive occasions, verses were put into valentine boxes. Each gentleman drew a lady's name and a verse, and read the verse to his lady.

If a man gave his sweetheart a pair of gloves, he was asking for her hand in marriage. This was a popular and romantic way to propose.

One seventeenth-century poem begins:

> Go little gloves, salute my valentine.
> Which was, which is, which must and shall be
> mine. . . .

Wealthy English and Frenchmen gave their ladies rings, lockets, and other valentine jewelry. Others gave whatever gifts they could afford.

The custom of sending costly presents generally stopped around 1760. A few men, however, still declared their love with expensive presents on Valentine's Day. But by the late eighteenth century, valentine letters, romantic poems, and handmade love-tokens had replaced higher priced gifts.

Other popular love-tokens besides gloves were ladies' garters, paperweights, and scrimshaw (carvings or engravings made from tusk or bone). Sailors at sea made scrimshaw scenes for their sweethearts and inscribed them with loving messages. Women embroidered their initials on small pieces of silk or satin the size of pocket watches. They also embroidered the date and a romantic saying such as "Forever Yours." Men put these silk and satin pieces inside watchcases to keep out dust.

Anything given with love was an acceptable valentine gift. But gradually customs changed and people began to put their romantic feelings in writing.

3

PAPER VALENTINES
IN ENGLAND

In the Middle Ages sweethearts said—and sometimes sang—valentine verses to one another. Gradually, as people learned to read and write, valentines came to be love messages written on a sheet of paper. Some valentines were in letter form. Others were verses or poems.

The oldest paper valentine believed to exist is kept in the British Museum. It was written in 1415 by a Frenchman, Charles, the Duke of Orleans, who was captured by the British in the Battle of Agincourt. While Charles was in prison in the Tower of London, he wrote romantic verses to his wife. Many were written in French, but there are a few verses written in English that mention St. Valentine.

The first verse of one rhymed love letter written by Charles says:

> Wilt thou be mine? dear love, reply,
> Sweetly consent, or else deny:

Whisper softly, none shall know,
Wilt thou be mine, love? ay or no?

Paper valentines became popular in Europe and especially in England. Many of England's famous writers wrote valentine poems.

One English writer, Samuel Pepys, said in his diary that his wife had received a handmade valentine written with gold ink, on blue paper, from a young boy. It was one of the earliest of "modern" valentines.

In Europe, in the eighteenth century, it was the custom when calling on friends to write a message on a small card called a *visiting card*. The visiting cards developed into specially printed friendship or lovers' cards. Carefully designed by artists, they had borders of cupids, flowers, and birds. Their centers were left blank for messages. These cards were used in France and Germany on such special occasions as New Year's Day.

About this time in England there was a great demand for fancy bordered German paper. Beautifully decorated with pastel flowers and winged cupids, the paper was perfect for valentine letters. But it was very expensive. So, English firms began making their own paper with ornamental edges similar to the German paper and the lovers' cards.

Because it was so expensive to mail letters, a young man usually delivered his valentine to his sweetheart's home. Imagine the delight of a young woman who found a paper cutout heart hanging on her doorknob. It meant that a love letter had been slipped under the door.

The first printed valentines were printed from copperplate around 1800. They consisted of a single sheet of paper with a picture hand-painted or printed in the center. Most of

If V 2 I, as I 2 V am true,

V must lye, and

Thoughts——⎱
Searching ⎰ c
Valued ⎱
Love———⎰ may   B

 Truth never ties
Too A foole yy

If have part   W·R

And   IF   V bb

Y'have 1. 2. many then I. C.
And R not worth

Write⎱   QQ
I'le———⎰ not yours VV

them were trimmed with satin ribbons and had real lace borders. There was usually a space for people to write verses about their feelings.

Those who had no writing talent copied verses from little books called *valentine writers*. These booklets cost a penny. One was "The People's Valentine Writer, by a Literary Lady."

In the writers, there were sentimental poems and comic, even insulting verses. There were verses for sailors, soldiers, lonely people, the married, the unmarried, the young, and the old. Poems could be found for such occupations as hatter, milkman, butcher, and cheesemonger. Although the valentine writers were widely used, some people didn't like them because the verses were not original.

This valentine marriage proposal to a widow was in "The Polite Valentine Writer," published in London around 1820.

> *A widower to a widow sues*
> *And hopes his suit she'll not refuse.*
> *You have a child and so have I,*
> *They may cement affection's tie.*
> *Our fortunes I believe are equal,*
> *Let's join to make a pleasing sequel,*
> *At least this is my fond design,*
> *If you consent, dear Valentine.*

To reply, the widow could choose a verse of acceptance or of refusal from the valentine writer.

An early rebus (see page 25) of 1641 taken from Witt's Recreations

By about 1815, the cost of mailing a letter to someone in the same town had dropped to a penny. People no longer had to deliver their valentines to friends and neighbors in person. They could send them. Since the valentines were single sheets of paper, they were folded and sealed with reddish wax. Envelopes, then known as *paper pockets*, were not widely used because they doubled the cost of postage.

February 14 became one of the post office's busiest days. On Valentine's Day, young people waited anxiously for the letter carrier's knock. If they didn't get a valentine they were unhappy, and all the neighbors were sure to know.

At that time, it was usually the person who received the letter who paid the postage. If a valentine was insulting, the person who got it sometimes asked for his or her money back. The postmaster would read the valentine to decide if the money should be returned!

Later, the style of valentines changed to printed folders. Pictures of lovers, birds, cupids, and flowers were drawn on the front. People wrote verses inside.

In 1840, a new postal law allowed people to send a letter not only in their town, but anywhere in Great Britain and Ireland for one penny. With cheaper postage, Valentine's Day became more popular than ever.

Now, almost everyone used envelopes. Smaller, beautifully decorated printed valentines were made with matching envelopes. The first envelopes were manufactured without gum. In order to fasten them, each of four flaps had to be sealed

An English rhymed
valentine from
about 1850

INNOCENCE

When man was first from Eden driven,
By fiat from offended Heaven,
The Angels sought their homes above,
But left their essence, which was Love,
Which still as pure as at its birth,
Is to be found upon the Earth,
So if the bliss of Heaven youd prove,
Tis found in Innocence & Love

WHITE   DAISY

with colored bits of paper called *wafers*. These wafers had printed mottos, much like the stickers we have today. Later, when envelopes had gummed flaps, these little wafers were still popular.

The discovery of how to make paper lace brought about a big change in valentines. Joseph Addenbrooke was working for Dobbs, a London paper maker, when by chance he rubbed a metal tool with many small cutting ridges over an embossed, or raised design, on a piece of paper. The small holes that were left made the paper look like real lace. This lace looked so delicate that people had to feel it to see if it was real. Joseph Addenbrooke decided to go into business and make this new product.

Following his lead, other English factories began making beautiful paper lace copied from real lace designs. This was done by running long strips of paper through big rollers. The rollers stamped a lacy pattern on the paper's edges. Then the strips were cut into smaller pieces for valentines.

For about the next twenty years, English valentine makers turned out the fanciest, laciest valentines of all time. Many of them are so beautiful that they are on display in museums.

Even today, collectors look for valentines made between 1840 and 1860 because they are so lovely. These cards are called Victorian valentines because they were made during the period when Queen Victoria ruled Great Britain.

On Victorian valentines, paper lace was usually the background for a colorful picture, such as lovers in a garden or a fat cupid sitting on a satin pillow. Workers sewed or pasted hand-painted birds, hearts, or flowers onto the picture and lace. All the verses were carefully handwritten.

Jonathan King and his wife, Clarissa, were famous Victorian valentine makers. Their valentines were expensive, but people who could afford them thought they were worth the price. At the King Company, there was a special room for customers, who were mostly women, to choose their valentines in private.

Most of the valentines had two or three layers of delicate paper lace hinged together with paper "springs." The center was open, framing a beautiful handcolored picture.

Sometimes ornaments of velvet, brocade, satin, silk, or net were sewed on each layer of lace. Jonathan and Clarissa even used cloth roses made by nuns that looked and felt real. Every single flower petal, every feather of a bird's wing or tail was put on by hand. Clarissa was the first to apply tinsel to feathers and birds on her valentines. She even made glittering tinsel by powdering broken colored glass.

Some of the Jonathan King Company valentines had as many as seven hundred separate pieces. Their most spectacular creation was one unusual valentine with three thousand pieces!

As time went on, manufacturers found better ways to print color. Marcus Ward & Company became known for the quality of color in their cards.

Catherine "Kate" Greenaway and Walter Crane were well-known English artists who designed valentines for Marcus Ward & Company. Walter was a painter and book illustrator with great style. His valentines showed boys in knee breeches and elegant ladies in draped gowns.

Kate Greenaway was only in her twenties when she sold her first valentine design. She was paid fifteen dollars. The design sold twenty-five thousand copies in a few weeks. Sometimes Kate made costumes for dolls and painted pictures of them for her valentines. Although Kate drew flowers and landscapes, she is most famous for her children's book illustrations. Her charming sketches showed children dressed in quaint old-fashioned clothes.

Valentine styles kept changing. Card makers were always looking for new and different ideas. One novel valentine had a small *puzzle purse* in the center. It was like a square envelope with four flaps folded one inside the other. Verses were written on the folds, and there was a picture inside. The valentine was hard to read, but the worst part was folding the whole thing back up along the original folds.

Another English novelty was a valentine "marriage license" signed by Reverend Tie-Them-Tight. The reverend's name meant that he was tying the couple together in marriage.

One valentine card had a paper-lace envelope that held a lock of hair. Another had a small package of perfume. On one valentine, the verse was written upside down. There were even Braille valentines for the blind.

Sometimes valentines had moving parts. A piece of cardboard on the back of the card controlled the part that moved. If an arm moved, there might be a box of candy or a valentine underneath it. On one valentine, a church door opened, revealing a couple getting married.

Boldly colored comic valentines that made fun of people were popular during this time. The pictures were usually *caricatures*, figures that looked like cartoon drawings. One artist drew men with insect bodies and women with heads of birds. The verses were insulting and often rude. Some made fun of people's noses, or fat stomachs, their habits, or their work.

This comic valentine was sent to a girl who worried too much about her looks:

> 'Tis all in vain your simpering looks
> You never can incline
> With all your bustles, stays and curls
> To find a valentine.

Women and girls were hired by card companies to make valentines. The King factory at one time employed thirty girls to do the slow, tiresome handwork. They worked long hours for little pay, and they turned out beautiful cards.

In order to keep up with the demand for valentines, manufacturers looked for ways to speed up the work. Around 1880, many card makers began stamping pictures and ornaments on valentines by machine—a cheaper and faster method. Valentines were made with coarse paper lace trimmed with gaudy, fake jewels and ornaments such as berries and beads. There was no more delicate handwork. Machine-made cards were so cheap they sold for pennies.

People didn't like the cheap valentines and stopped buying them. The newspapers often wrote about how useless and vulgar they were. To stimulate business, some manufacturers tried to go back to making elegant, expensive valentines with silk-fringed edges. They made cards folded in two with silk cords or tassels so they would be easy to open. But most English people had lost interest in Valentine's Day. Very few continued the custom of exchanging cards. By the end of World War I, in 1918, the only valentines popular in England were mechanical and trick types, mostly for children.

Then in 1925, a greeting card firm owned by Sir Adolph Tuck was having a diamond jubilee. Lady Jeanetta Tuck suggested to her husband that they might celebrate the occasion by reviving the custom of sending valentines.

The next year, the Tuck firm brought valentines back to the English public. Other manufacturers began making valentines again, and the British Post Office helped by issuing valentine telegrams.

St. Valentine's Day and its customs were restored with enthusiasm in England. The British still celebrate the holiday today by sending valentine cards to one another.

]19[

A Pennsylvania Dutch betrothal letter from about 1743

4

THE STORY OF
AMERICAN VALENTINES

The early American settlers often received valentines from friends in England and other European countries. But they were too busy clearing land and building homes to make many valentines themselves. Few girls in the colonies followed the European custom of using magic spells and charms to guess who their future husbands would be. Besides, the Puritans in the Massachusetts Bay Colony who were deeply religious, thought Valentine's Day was a frivolous holiday. They didn't participate in Valentine's Day celebrations or customs.

It wasn't until the middle of the eighteenth century, about one hundred years after the founding of the Massachusetts Bay Colony, that Americans began sending valentines to one another. Most valentines were proposals of marriage from men to their sweethearts. Young farmers spent long winter nights practicing penmanship and writing poems in different styles and designs. Many of these handmade valentines were treasured and saved. Sometimes, a young woman would answer a proposal of marriage with a valentine.

It took a lot of work and imagination to make a valentine. Valentines with a lacy look and cutouts were popular. To make a cutout, paper was folded several times and a design of birds, flowers, or hearts was cut with a sharp scissors. Cutouts were often in the form of a *True-Love Knot*. The True-Love or *Endless-Love Knot* was usually a hand-drawn, hand-colored maze, sometimes forming a pattern such as interlocking hearts. The verses written inside the complicated paths had no beginning and no end. The message could be read beginning at random from any line. The valentines were often bordered with flowers and cupids. They weren't easy to make, and those who received them spent a long time figuring them out.

Among the popular valentines of the day were delicate handmade pin-pricked designs. Pictures such as houses, trees, or the hands and faces of men and women would be painted on the valentines. The people's clothing, or perhaps a bird in the tree, and the fancy border around the picture would be pricked out by pins and needles of different sizes to give a raised or embossed effect. Imagine how many holes were needed to make a frame around a large valentine!

Puzzle-style valentines were fun. Below is an *acrostic* valentine proposal to a girl named Mary. In this kind of puzzle the first letter of each line spells her name.

> **M**ay you answer, "Yes," my heart
> **A**nd no longer keep us apart
> **R**emember I love you, dear Valentine
> **Y**ou must be mine as I am thine.

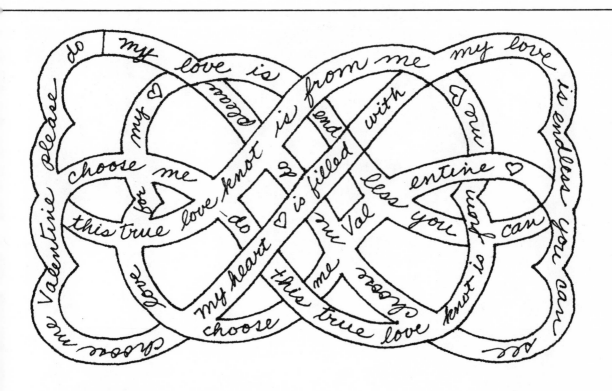

This true love knot is from me.
My love is endless you can see
Choose me valentine please do
My heart is filled with love for you!

True-love, or endless-love knot

Some valentines copied the English puzzle-purse. Instead of putting a picture inside, some creative valentine makers put interesting items such as a lock of hair or a ring in the center.

The *rebus*, another puzzle-type valentine, was like the puzzle purse. The verses were usually numbered and written on paper folded every which way. When the valentine was opened there was often a painted picture in the center. Some rebus valentines had a tiny picture in place of a word:

Nobody   ⌐   how much   👁   🌲   4   U   dear

Theorem or *Poonah* valentines were done in an Oriental style of painting. All the outlines and designs were drawn or traced on oil paper. They were cut out to form what is called a *stencil*. Watercolors were painted on through the holes in the stencil. Then the design was coated with gum arabic to fix the color. The same type of method was used to paint on velvet.

Another kind of valentine was the old-fashioned *tintype*, which was a photograph taken on a special sheet of tin or iron. A tintype picture of a young man or his sweetheart was put in the center of fancy writing paper. Decorations were painted or pasted on by hand.

The popular *fractur* style was brought to America by Ger-

A Poonah valentine
from about 1845

man immigrants who settled in Pennsylvania. Fractur valentines were usually proposals of marriage. The birds, flowers, and hearts on these valentines were mostly colored in brilliant reds, blues, yellows, and greens. The ornamental lettering, which resembled manuscripts of the Middle Ages, was magnificent. Because of their superior workmanship, valentines made by the Pennsylvania Germans are prized by modern collectors.

With the coming of the Machine Age, American valentine makers began turning out machine-printed valentines. Some were engraved or made from woodcuts. Most were printed and hand-colored. A blank space was left for the sender to write a message. Valentine writer booklets were used in America as well as in England as a source for verses.

American men delivered their valentines just as men in Britain did. Then, in 1845, a cheaper postal rate was set for the entire country. Because it cost less to mail valentines, many more people sent them, and the popularity of valentines soared. Although some valentines were still made by hand until the late 1880s, card makers couldn't keep up with the demand for their machine-made valentines.

The cupids, flowers, and other handmade decorations gave American valentines a certain charm. But even the expensive ones didn't compare with the beauty of British Victorian valentines. American valentine paper was coarse-grained. It couldn't be used for embossing or stamping out delicate lace.

Esther Howland, an energetic young woman from Worcester, Massachusetts, is credited with starting the fancy valentine business in America. She was a college graduate at a time when few women had the chance for a higher education. Soon after graduation in 1847, her father, who owned a large book and stationery store, imported a few English valentines. They were made of fine paper lace and colored flowers. Esther had never seen such beautiful valentines.

Esther was artistic, and she told her father she was sure she could make lacy valentines that would be just as pretty as the English ones—maybe prettier. Mr. Howland agreed to let her try.

Esther cut out designs from decorated envelopes. She pasted the designs and several colored pictures onto sheets of paper. Then she scalloped the edges of the paper. One of her brothers wrote verses in elegant handwriting. The valentines were so lovely that her father sold them in his shop.

Esther made a few dozen more, and another brother took them along to sell on a business trip. In just weeks he sold thousands of dollars worth of Esther's valentines to stores. She had enough orders to keep her busy for years!

Showing good business sense, Esther asked her father to order more material to make valentines. Then she hired several friends and set up a workroom in her home. Each worker had a job. Esther designed the cards. One woman cut out pictures. Another pasted a picture onto paper. The next woman pasted tiny paper flowers onto the paper lace. The background was painted by another. A tiny red letter H, for Howland, was written on the back of the card. Esther had what we now call an assembly line. Since each young woman did only one special job, she was able to do it better and faster than if she made an entire valentine. Every single valentine order was filled on time.

The women enjoyed working for Esther. She paid them well. The next year, the demand for valentines doubled. Esther hired more women. The third floor of her home was now a valentine factory. Orders continued to pour in, and the factory moved to larger quarters.

By the end of 1849, Esther Howland was running a big business. In those days it was rare for a woman to run a business. Esther's factory had a good reputation. She thought of many new ideas. One was to place a small colored paper wafer as backing under the lace paper on her cards. Her valentines were also the first to have printed verses on the inside page.

Howland valentines sold for between five and ten dollars. Some cost as much as thirty-five dollars. Although they were expensive, business boomed. For a long time, Esther Howland owned the only American factory that made lacy valentines. It is not surprising that her business grew until it earned over one hundred thousand dollars a year—a lot of money in those days.

In 1880, Esther sold out to George C. Whitney, who was also from Worcester. He, too, became an important valentine maker. His business survived many years of changing styles. In 1942, when the Whitney Company closed its doors, there had been almost a century of valentine making in Worcester, Massachusetts.

Louis Prang, along with Esther Howland and George C. Whitney, was also a pioneer in the American greeting card industry. He started his manufacturing company in 1860, and quickly became famous for valentines with clear, printed

An Esther Howland valentine
with a satin back and
ornaments made in Germany,
mounted on embossed paper

Faithful

This Louis Prang valentine was made around 1880.

designs done in vivid color. Sometimes he used as many as twenty colors on a card. For trimming, Louis Prang used silk fringe instead of paper lace. He was the first manufacturer to use verses printed directly on the cards.

During the Civil War years soldiers and their families exchanged many patriotic and sentimental valentines. One popular valentine at that time showed a flag-draped tent. When the tent flaps were opened there was a soldier pictured writing a love verse to his sweetheart. Envelopes for sentimental valentines were delicately embossed or printed.

Other valentines of that time were political, and many were comic. Comics sold for a penny each and were called *penny dreadfuls*. One comic valentine published by the New York Union Valentine Company showed two ladies staring at a conceited soldier. The first verse says:

> *You are a gallant soldier,*
> *With a splendid figure for parade;*
> *The country is safe in your keeping*
> *So long as you fight in the shade.*

In the years after the Civil War, comic valentine verses became more and more insulting, and senders rarely signed them. Comic valentine manufacturers competed for customers. They turned out valentines as fast and cheaply as possible and could barely keep up with the demand.

American interest in the sentimental valentine continued into the 1880s and 1890s. The style hadn't changed much from earlier years. Valentines usually had a colored embossed background and a fancy layer or two of pretty paper with a delicate design. The corners were decorated with small flowers or cupids. Fancy open work or lace paper was backed by colored paper for contrast. Cards were large—sometimes 11 inches (28 cm) long, and 8 inches (20 cm) wide.

Then the style of American valentines changed. Around the beginning of the twentieth century people stopped buying sentimental valentines and became interested in novelties. They liked valentines that featured children. But the most popular novelties of the time were bright-colored valentines from Germany. They came folded flat, in all sizes and shapes. They were opened by pulling paper springs that were attached. And with the help of a cardboard backrest the valentines could stand on a mantel or table.

The car had just been invented, and people were fascinated by mechanical car valentines. On some cards, the wheels actually moved. One popular valentine was a car with a chubby little Cupid in the driver's seat.

About 1907, postcard valentines printed in Germany were in fashion in America. People collected them and pasted them in albums. It wasn't unusual for families to have several albums filled with postcards of cupids and red satin hearts.

Americans stopped buying German valentines during World War I because the United States was at war with Germany. Although there wasn't a great demand for valentines at this time, interest in Valentine's Day never completely died in America as it had in England. Manufacturers managed to turn out valentines in spite of the war and a paper shortage. Women sent valentines to their husbands and sweethearts in the armed forces, keeping the industry going.

An American valentine
from the Gay Nineties

GREETING TO MY LOVE.

Between 1906 and 1919, all the major card companies in business today were started: Hallmark, Norcross, Gibson, American Greetings, and Rust Craft.

After World War I, most Americans seemed to prefer things streamlined and modern. The language of valentine verses changed to keep up with the times. Card makers no longer used verses such as:

> *Dear valentine I love thee*
> *Pray tell if thou lovest me.*

The "thees" and "thous" disappeared and were replaced by everyday language:

> *I like your looks and your style*
> *For you, valentine, I'd walk a mile.*

When the Great Depression came in 1929 there were hard times in America. Many people lost their jobs, and some lost their life savings, but they managed to scrape up money to buy valentines. Card makers continued to manufacture them and they survived the financial crisis.

During World War II, the greeting card business became an important American industry. Women had always sent val-

A German postcard
valentine made by the
Obpacher Brothers
around 1880

entines to those in military service. Now those in the service sent valentines home, too.

In the 1950s, the shape of valentine cards changed. Long, narrow, Studio Cards were in style. They were sometimes funny, and sometimes uncomplimentary. In the sixties, most people passed up Studio Cards for more casual sentiments. This one is quite simple:

Just dropping by
With a valentine Hi.

Young people in the seventies felt the need for tenderness and love. A typical seventies valentine might say:

I offer my love for you to keep
My feeling is sincere and deep.

A romantic valentine didn't always rhyme. This one says:

How do I love you? . . . Sincerely!

These cards were often illustrated with romantic, color photographs of couples walking in a meadow or standing on a hill.

In spite of wars, the Depression, and changing styles and tastes, valentines are still very much alive in America.

Norcross made this
valentine around 1918.

5

VALENTINE'S DAY
TODAY

Today, in celebration of Valentine's Day, children of Great Britain get candy or money for singing songs. Some English people bake special valentine buns with raisins, caraway seeds, or plum filling. In Italy, St. Valentine's Day is a feast day.

German manufacturers began making valentines again after World War II, when American soldiers stationed there wanted them to send home. Valentine's Day is still observed in parts of Germany, Austria, and Spain. But it is mostly people in the United States and Canada who celebrate St. Valentine's Day. Except for Christmas, Americans send more cards on Valentine's Day than any other day. Americans also buy more valentines than all other countries combined.

Valentines can be bought individually or in boxes. They can also be made from special kits, or created from doilies, wallpaper, or construction paper and decorated with pictures from magazines.

Modern card manufacturers give their valentines special care and attention. A great deal of time is spent in planning, researching, and writing before a valentine is put on store shelves. The Hallmark Company says as many as ninety-five working days are needed to turn out a greeting card, from first step to last.

Card manufacturers don't paste and sew decorations on valentines by hand anymore. They use advanced machines and equipment to carry out the artist's idea. Today's valentines go through many processes. They may be dyed different colors, laminated with thin layers of material, flocked or coated with finely powdered wool or cloth, embossed in raised designs, or printed. Sometimes they are made to look like leather, wood, or some type of metal. They no longer have rose petals that look and feel real. But there are colored threads, diamond dust sequins, and other beautiful trimmings put on by machine.

Card makers buy verses from professional writers or from amateurs, who occasionally come up with good ideas. Hallmark Cards receives as many as seventy thousand valentine ideas in one year.

Although there are company art directors, planners, and editorial directors who work on a card, each idea is also tested for public reaction. A valentine with several different designs and verses might be brought to a church group, a PTA, or a university class. The group is asked to give their opinions on the different combinations of designs and verses. If enough people approve of a design, the valentine card goes on to the next step. Sometimes the creators have to go back to their typewriters and drawing boards and start all over.

When an idea passes all reviewers and a card has been designed, there are thirty testing stations before final approval. At each step, the card is studied carefully and a decision is reached, such as the envelope size, how to fold the valentine, a background color, a type of paper (parchment, tissue, or rough), or a price. The card may be classified as general, religious, juvenile, humorous, or some other category. Then it is tested for quality, whether its price is twenty-five cents or one dollar.

Higher-priced novelties such as valentine figurines, stuffed toys, booklets of love poems, and sentimental messages printed on wood, fill the stores around February 14, too.

Valentine's Day is no longer just for sweethearts. In fact, children send more valentines than adults. Boys and girls give loving valentines to their parents, grandparents, relatives, and friends. A valentine to your mother and dad might say:

> *Here's to parents who are loving*
> *In everything they do*
> *Parents who are very special*
> *My PARENTS—that's who!*

There are valentines for teachers:

> *I like you a lot, TEACHER, under any condition*
> *But I won't speak out without permission.*

A valentine to a cousin or friend might have this verse:

> *With friendly, happy thoughts*
> *This is coming your way*
> *To say hello and tell you*
> *Happy Valentine's Day.*

People love to poke fun at one another. This comic valentine is from a girl to a boy:

Hickory dickory dock
Your face would stop a clock.

In contrast to the fancy lace valentines of the Victorian times, today's valentines are simple, yet attractive. The language is different, but the message is the same. "I'm thinking of you. Happy Valentine's Day."

6

VALENTINE SYMBOLS

A chubby, golden-winged cupid carrying a bow and a quiver of arrows stands for St. Valentine's Day. So do flowers, paper-lace hearts, and love birds. These valentine decorations are symbols of love and affection. They each have a special meaning.

In days past, many a cutout lace heart decorated with flowers and birds was given as a love token. Later, when paper valentines replaced love tokens these decorations were pasted, or sewn on valentines by hand. Since then, they've been printed and hand-painted, and later manufactured by machine. Other symbols have come and gone, but hearts, flowers, birds, and cupids have continued from ancient times until this very day.

Around February 14, hearts, the most common symbol of romantic love, are seen everywhere. Shops sell chocolates in red satin heart boxes, and we see tiny pastel candy hearts with sayings such as "Be Mine." Lockets and other heart-shaped jewelry are shown in store windows. There are even under-clothes and pajamas decorated with hearts.

Why is the heart a symbol of love? Probably because some primitive peoples thought our souls lived in our hearts. Others believed that human intelligence came from the heart. Even today, we call someone "heartless," or say something is "heart-warming," or that we are "broken-hearted," as if our hearts had feelings.

Perhaps the heart is associated with love because it was Cupid's (a Greek god's) target. The legend says that anyone hit by Cupid's bow will fall helplessly in love.

Long ago, a young man would write a verse offering his heart to his valentine. Today, the custom still goes on, and it probably will for years to come.

Flowers have been valentine symbols for a long time. We all know verses that begin:

Roses are red
Violets are blue . . .

According to ancient legends and myths people have always associated delicate, sweet-smelling flowers with love. When Valentine, the priest, was in prison, children threw him bou-quets of flowers as a sign of love. Later, young men gave their ladies flowers as love tokens at name drawings.

Today, the custom of sending flowers to say, "I love you," has spread from the United States and England to other parts of Europe.

There is no special flower associated with Valentine's Day.

Yet through the years the rose has been a favorite symbol of love. Perhaps it is because in flower language, a red rose means "I love you." Red is thought of as the most romantic color, the color of the human heart.

Carnations in various hues of pink were often used with roses to decorate valentines. They were drawn or painted on by hand. Valentines today still have floral decorations, along with the other valentine symbols.

Birds, symbols of spring and mating, were common on early, handmade valentines. This was probably because of the old belief that birds choose their mates on St. Valentine's Day.

In a work by the English poet Chaucer, one stanza says:

For this was on St. Valentine's Day
When every fowl cometh to choose his mate . . .

Sometimes delicate lace valentines pictured birds building nests. Pennsylvania Germans made fine cutouts with hand-colored birds in the corners. Pairs of doves were often drawn on valentines, too. But sometimes, there was only one dove shown carrying a love letter. Doves have been thought of as messengers since ancient times. Because doves make gentle, cooing sounds we often say they "bill and coo." This has become a romantic term. One hand-painted valentine watch paper shows two fluttering doves, their heads entwined in a wedding ring.

Probably another reason that there are doves on valentines is that in the past they were considered magical. Some people thought that a flock of doves overhead meant good luck in marriage. Others believed that to dream of a dove was a promise of happiness.

Pairs of small parrots with vivid green, orange, and purple feathers are also used as valentine ornaments. Because the parrots pair off and leave the other birds, they're often called lovebirds. It's no wonder they were chosen to decorate valentines.

Cupid, the symbol of love and happiness, is perhaps the most famous valentine symbol of all. The chubby figure with the bow and arrow has lasted through many changes in valentine styles. He is really the spirit of St. Valentine's Day.

Stories of Cupid go back to the ancient Greek myths, in which he was called Eros. He was the son of Aphrodite, the goddess of love and beauty, and Mars, the god of war. The Romans called him Cupid, and his mother, Venus.

Cupid was a happy little god who stayed near his mother. He wanted others to be happy too, so he shot his gold-tipped invisible arrows into their hearts and made them fall in love.

According to one well-known Greek myth, Venus was jealous of a mortal princess named Psyche because she was very beautiful. Venus ordered Cupid to either kill Psyche, or to make her fall in love with the most horrible creature in the world.

Cupid took his arrows and some poison and went to look for Psyche. But when he saw her beauty, he was so stunned, he fell on one of his own love arrows. Love for Psyche filled his heart to overflowing. He married her and brought her to his palace to live. Because Psyche was human, she was not allowed to see what he looked like.

Psyche was content with her life in the palace until her two older sisters came to visit. They saw all the beautiful treasures that Psyche had, and they were on fire with jealousy. When Psyche confessed to them that she'd never seen her husband they convinced her that she'd married a serpent who was going to kill her. They advised her to kill him before it was too late.

Psyche protested that she loved her husband. But did she? Her sisters said he was a serpent. It might be true. She had better kill him. But could she? Not until she saw what he looked like.

That night, when Cupid was asleep, Psyche went into his room with an oil lamp and a dagger. When the light touched his face she saw that her husband was not a monster. He was young and handsome. She was very relieved. But her hand shook, and a drop of oil hit Cupid's shoulder. He awakened, saw the dagger in her hand, and scolded her. Then he told her who he was and said, "Love cannot live where there is no trust." Without another word, he disappeared, and so did the palace and everything around it!

Psyche found herself standing in an open meadow. She cried. She knew now that she really loved her husband and would spend the rest of her life searching for him. She looked everywhere, but Cupid was nowhere to be found. Finally, she went to Venus and begged the goddess to help her.

Venus promised to help if Psyche performed several dangerous tasks. She hoped harm would come to Psyche, because she actually hated the girl.

Each task was harder than the one before. But Psyche did them with the help of insects and beasts who loved her. Finally, there was only one task left. Psyche was to go to the underworld and bring back a box filled with the beauty ointment of Proserpina, the wife of Pluto, the god of the underworld.

A voice told Psyche how to find the box and warned her of terrible danger if she looked inside. But when Psyche found the box, she couldn't resist opening it. Immediately, she fell into a deep sleep.

Cupid, still in love with her, flew to her and woke her with a kiss. He explained to her that she was a mortal and could never discover the beauty of goddesses.

Cupid begged Jupiter, king of the gods, to command Venus to forgive them for getting married. Jupiter did so, and soon after, he made Psyche a goddess. Cupid and Psyche lived happily on Olympus.

Cupid is thought to represent the heart, and Psyche the soul. Through the years, the little god has become the symbol of love that decorates today's valentines.

Chubby cupids, lacy red hearts, pink flowers, and lovebirds add more frills to an already frivolous holiday. But perhaps Valentine's Day has a deeper meaning than the coming of spring, and the mating of birds, and people falling in love.

People have sent valentine messages to one another for almost two thousand years. Valentine's Day proves that even in our modern world, we still believe in love and friendship.

7

VALENTINE
FUN

People have celebrated Valentine's Day with parties and dances since the ancient Roman festival of Lupercalia. The Romans wore costumes and masks. There were name-drawings, and love tokens were exchanged.

Children in the nineteenth century also had parties. They gave each other valentines, played games, and ate heart-shaped sweets. Sometimes they played *Drop the Handkerchief*, a circle game where a girl drops a hanky behind a boy. He chases her and gets a kiss—if he catches her. Early in the twentieth century there were parties, refreshments, and games also.

Young people in America still have parties to celebrate St. Valentine's Day. Food, games, and choosing partners are all part of the fun. There are usually heart-shaped valentine decorations in pink and red and valentine boxes (made out of boxes) covered with red crepe paper and white lace doilies.

Here are some suggestions for food and games at a valentine get-together.

TABLE CENTERPIECE

Insert straws on which red paper hearts are taped into a small plant. Or make a valentine tree from a tree branch. Tape valentines on it.

FOOD

Make your own peanut butter and jelly sandwiches. Cut off crusts of sliced bread. Use a heart-shaped cookie cutter to cut hearts. Spread on the peanut butter and jelly.

Or: Make your own pizza. Buy prepared pizza crust, canned pizza sauce, and grated mozarella cheese. Cut the dough in heart shapes with a cookie cutter. Have your guests make their own pizzas.

Heart-Shaped Finger Jello

4 cups boiling water
4 envelopes Knox gelatin
3 pkgs. (3 ounces) red jello

Mix the jello and gelatin. Add boiling water and stir until dissolved. Pour the liquid into a 3-quart oblong casserole. Let it set for several hours. When jelled, use a cookie cutter to make heart shapes. Jello can be picked up with fingers. Makes 12.

Never-Fail Heart-Shaped Sugar Cookies

1½ cups sifted confectioners sugar
1 cup butter or margarine
1 egg

1 teaspoon vanilla
1/2 teaspoon almond flavoring
2 1/2 cups flour
1 teaspoon baking soda
1 teaspoon cream of tartar

Mix the ingredients. Wrap the dough in plastic wrap and re-frigerate for 2–3 hours. Roll out small amounts of dough at a time. Cut with heart-shaped cookie cutter and sprinkle with red-colored sugar or red hearts. Bake at 375° for 7–8 minutes. Cool on wire rack and enjoy!

Percolator Punch (Serve hot or cold)

Fill a 30-cup percolator with:
2 32-ounce cans of cranberry juice cocktail
1 46-ounce can of unsweetened pineapple juice
1 cup brown sugar

In basket put:
4 teaspoons whole cloves
12 sticks cinnamon (broken)
Peel of 1/4 orange—cut in strips

Perk as you would for coffee. This can be made ahead and stored in refrigerator. Makes 12–18 cups.

More Nutritious Food Ideas

Appetizer: Add pimento pieces to sour cream onion dip. Garnish with cherry tomatoes.

Fruit: Use jellied cranberry sauce from a can. Cut in heart shapes with a cookie cutter.

Dessert: Make vanilla pudding and put red candy hearts on top.

Valentine Waldorf Salad

2 red apples coarsely diced
2 Tablespoons sugar
2 Tablespoons lemon juice
Dash of salt
1 cup sliced celery
1/2 cup chopped nuts
1/2 cup coarsely diced maraschino cherries
Mayonnaise

Sprinkle apples with sugar, lemon juice, and salt, mixing well. Add celery, nuts, and cherries. Stir in mayonnaise to moisten. Serves eight.

Valentine Kidney Bean Salad

1-pound can kidney beans
1/4 cup sweet onion diced
1/2 cup celery diced
1/4 cup sweet pickle relish
1/4 cup mayonnaise
1/4 cup half-and-half sour cream
1 Tablespoon lemon juice
1 Tablespoon vinegar
1 Tablespoon sugar
Salt and pepper to taste

Mix beans and onion in a large bowl. Combine next seven ingredients and blend well. Add to beans and mix gently, but thoroughly. Refrigerate overnight. You might need more salt or pepper. Serves eight.

GAMES

Famous Pairs

Pin a name on each guest's back. Tell him or her to ask questions of the other guests to discover who they are. When they do find out, they can look for their partner. Partners can be used for other games.

SUGGESTIONS:

Mickey Mouse and Minnie	Jack and Jill
Princess Leia and Luke Skywalker	Popeye and Olive Oyl
King and Queen of Hearts	Romeo and Juliet
Cinderella and the Prince	Donny and Marie
Raggedy Ann and Andy	Barbie Doll and Ken

If you don't want male and female partners, use names like Laurel and Hardy or Abbott and Costello.

Charades

Break up into teams. Put out a bowl of small candy hearts with mottoes, and cover it. Without looking, pick a candy heart. Act it out. The time limit for your team to guess is five minutes.

Make a Valentine Contest

Place doilies, construction paper, glitter, scissors, and paste on a table. Set a time limit of fifteen or twenty minutes to make a valentine. You can use partners. Whoever makes the most original valentine wins.

How Many Words Can You Make
Out of St. Valentine's Day?

You can use partners for this too.

VALENTINES

How to Make a Pinprick Valentine

YOU NEED:
1. A piece of white typing paper
2. A picture of large bird cut from a magazine if you can't draw one
3. Tracing paper if you trace your bird instead of drawing it
4. Pencil
5. Pen
6. Crayons
7. Pins and needles of different thicknesses

1. Draw or trace the picture of the bird a bit above center on the paper. Leave room for the verse or verses at the bottom and a margin of at least an inch (2.5 cm) at top and sides.
2. Draw trees or houses for a background and color with crayons.
3. Start with the thickest needle or pin and poke holes to outline the bird's body.
4. Then do another row inside of that row with the next size pin or needle.

Roses are red
Grass is green
You're the cutest girl
I've ever seen.

Be my valentine.
Love, Randy

Pinprick valentine

5. Continue this, alternating sizes of pins until you've finished the picture.
6. Make a pinprick border around the entire valentine in the same manner, alternating rows of thick and thin pins.
7. Write a valentine verse at the bottom in your best handwriting.
8. Be creative!

How To Make a Cutout Valentine

YOU NEED:
1. Pink or red construction paper
2. Sharp scissors
3. Pencil
4. Ruler
5. Paste
6. Crayons or felt-tip pens of different colors

OPTIONAL:
Paper-lace doilies, candy hearts, and scraps of ribbon, lace, yarn, or velvet, cutouts from old magazines and greeting cards.

1. Place the construction paper in a horizontal position. Fold it three times in the shape of a triangle (or a hat).
2. Open the paper. Starting 1 inch (2.5 cm) from the point at the top, draw a small heart with the pencil, so that the center is on the crease. Draw hearts all the way down, stopping 1 inch from the bottom. Leave 1/4 inch (.6 cm) of space between each heart. Repeat hearts on the other side. You should have room for about 8 to 10 hearts.

FOLD
LINES

BE MY
VALENTINE

Cutout valentine

3. Fold the paper into the triangle again. With a sharp scissors, cut out the hearts (actually, only half of each heart). When the paper is open, there will be cutout hearts on both sides.
4. In the center, below the point, paste a picture. Cut out a border around it. *Or*: Draw a flower or large heart in the center. Be sure to leave room at the bottom for the verse. Then, fold the paper down the center of the flower or heart. Cut it out.
5. Draw a heart or bird in each corner. Cut it out.
6. Scallop the edges around the valentine with your scissors. Or paste strips of paper lace from doilies around the edges.
7. Use crayons to draw in a background for your valentine. Paste on scraps of ribbon, velvet, and candy hearts to decorate.
8. Write a verse or message with a felt-tip pen.

How to Make a Paper Spring Valentine

YOU NEED:
1. Red or pink construction paper, or other fancy paper
2. Paste
3. Ruler
4. Crayons or colored felt-tip pens
5. A 4-inch by 4-inch (10-cm by 10-cm) picture cut from an old magazine or greeting card. Or draw your own.
6. Small pictures of hearts, birds, cupids, or other love tokens
7. White paper-lace doilies
8. Scissors

Paper spring valentine

1. Place the construction paper in a horizontal position. Paste a picture from a magazine or greeting card in the center of the paper. Or draw and color your own.
2. Draw a 1/2-inch (1.3-cm) border around the picture. Color it.
3. Cut paper doilies into 1/4-inch (.6-cm) strips. Paste them around the inside of the border.

MAKE THE PAPER SPRINGS:
1. Fold a piece of unlined writing paper lengthwise.
2. Fold it alternately backward and forward three times.
3. Cut the paper into 1/2-inch (1.3-cm) pieces.

PAPER SPRING

ATTACH PAPER SPRINGS TO VALENTINE:
1. Paste one end of each paper spring in the spaces between the picture in the center and the lace border.
2. On the other end of each spring paste a strip of plain, flat paper.
3. On these strips paste small flowers, birds, cupids, or hearts. The strips form a pretty stand-out frame around the picture, and the paper springs enable the valentine to be folded flat.
4. Write a valentine verse or greeting with a felt-tip pen or crayon.

BIBLIOGRAPHY

Encyclopedia Americana, Volume 27: 1981.

Engen, Rodney K. *Kate Greenaway*. London. Academy Editions, New York, Harmony Books, 1976.

Goeller, Carl G. *Writing and Selling Greeting Cards*. Boston: Writer, Inc., 1980.

Guerber, Helene A. *Myths of Greece and Rome*. New York: American Book Company, 1893.

Hallmark Cards, Incorporated. Kansas City, Missouri.

Hamilton, Edith. *Mythology*. New York: Little Brown and Co., 1942.

"Hearts and Flourishes: A Valentine Scrapbook," *The Saturday Review*, February 4, 1978.

Kaufmann, Patricia. "Saint Valentine's Love Note Started It," *Smithsonian*, February, 1976.

Lee, Ruth Webb. *A History of Valentines*. Wellesley Hills, Massachusetts: Lee Publications, 1952.

Man, Felix H. *Artists' Lithographs*. New York: G. P. Putnam's Sons, 1970.

Means, Carroll Alton. "Kate Greenaway's Valentines," *Hobbies*, February, 1953.

Schweitzer, John C. "Honoring Saint Valentine." *Hobbies*, February, 1976.

Staff, Frank. *The Picture Postcard and its Origins*. New York: Lutterworth Publications, 1966.

Staff, Frank. *The Valentine and its Origins*. New York: Praeger Publishing, Inc., 1969.

INDEX